Fascinating Insects
Moths

Aaron Carr

www.av2books.com

AV² provides enriched content that supplements and complements this book. Weigl's AV² books strive to create inspired learning and engage young minds in a total learning experience.

Your AV² Media Enhanced books come alive with...

Audio
Listen to sections of the book read aloud.

Video
Watch informative video clips.

Embedded Weblinks
Gain additional information for research.

Try This!
Complete activities and hands-on experiments.

Key Words
Study vocabulary, and complete a matching word activity.

Quizzes
Test your knowledge.

Slide Show
View images and captions, and prepare a presentation.

... and much, much more!

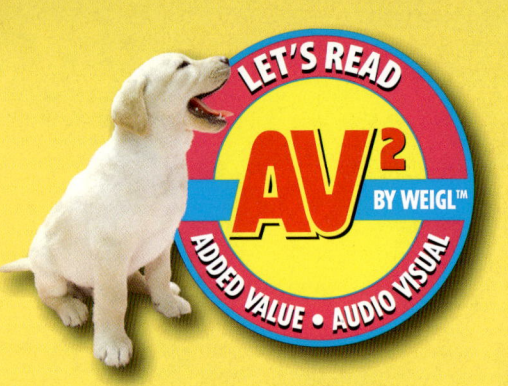

Go to www.av2books.com, and enter this book's unique code.

BOOK CODE

Y376348

AV² by Weigl brings you media enhanced books that support active learning.

Published by AV² by Weigl
350 5th Avenue, 59th Floor New York, NY 10118
Websites: www.av2books.com   www.weigl.com

Copyright ©2015 AV² by Weigl
All rights reserved. No part of this publication may be reproduced, stored in a retrieval system, or transmitted in any form or by any means, electronic, mechanical, photocopying, recording, or otherwise, without the prior written permission of the publisher.

Library of Congress Cataloging-in-Publication Data
Carr, Aaron.
  Moths / Aaron Carr.
      pages. cm -- (Fascinating insects)
  ISBN 978-1-4896-1042-3 (hardcover : alk. paper) -- ISBN 978-1-4896-1043-0 (softcover : alk. paper) --
  ISBN 978-1-4896-1044-7 (single-user ebook) -- ISBN 978-1-4896-1045-4 (multi-user ebook)
  1. Moths--Juvenile literature. I. Title.
  QL544.2.C367 2014
  595.78--dc23
                                                  2014002369

Printed in the United States of America in North Mankato, Minnesota
1 2 3 4 5 6 7 8 9 0 18 17 16 15 14

032014
WEP150314

Project Coordinator: Aaron Carr   Art Director: Terry Paulhus

Weigl acknowledges Getty Images as the primary image supplier for this title.

Moths

CONTENTS

2 AV² Book Code
4 Meet the Moth
6 Where They Live
8 Life Cycle
10 Caterpillars
12 Growing Up
14 How They Fly
16 How They See
18 How They Eat
20 Role in Nature
22 Moth Facts
24 Key Words/
AV2books.com

Meet the moth.

Moths are flying insects that look like butterflies.

Moths live in most parts of the world.

In most parts of the world, moths like to live in forest areas.

7

Moths are born
when they hatch from eggs.

When they hatch from eggs, moths look like long, furry worms.

Moths are called caterpillars when they are young.

When they are young, caterpillars spend most of their time eating.

Moth caterpillars wrap themselves in a bag of silk called a cocoon.

Inside a bag of silk called a cocoon, caterpillars grow into adult moths.

Moths have four wings when they are fully-grown.

When they are fully-grown, moths use their wings to fly and to hide from other animals.

Moths have two large eyes with many parts.

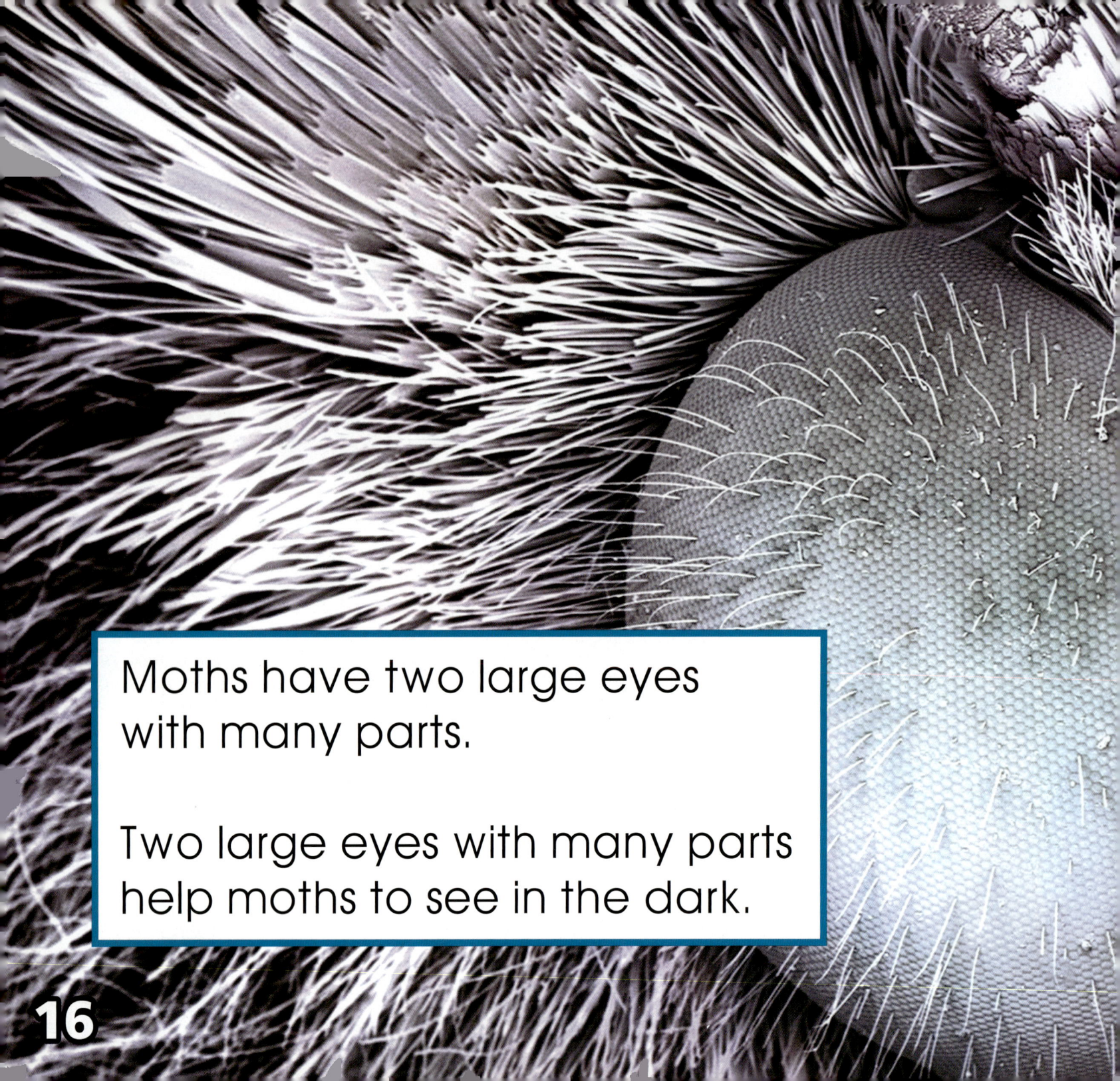

Two large eyes with many parts help moths to see in the dark.

17

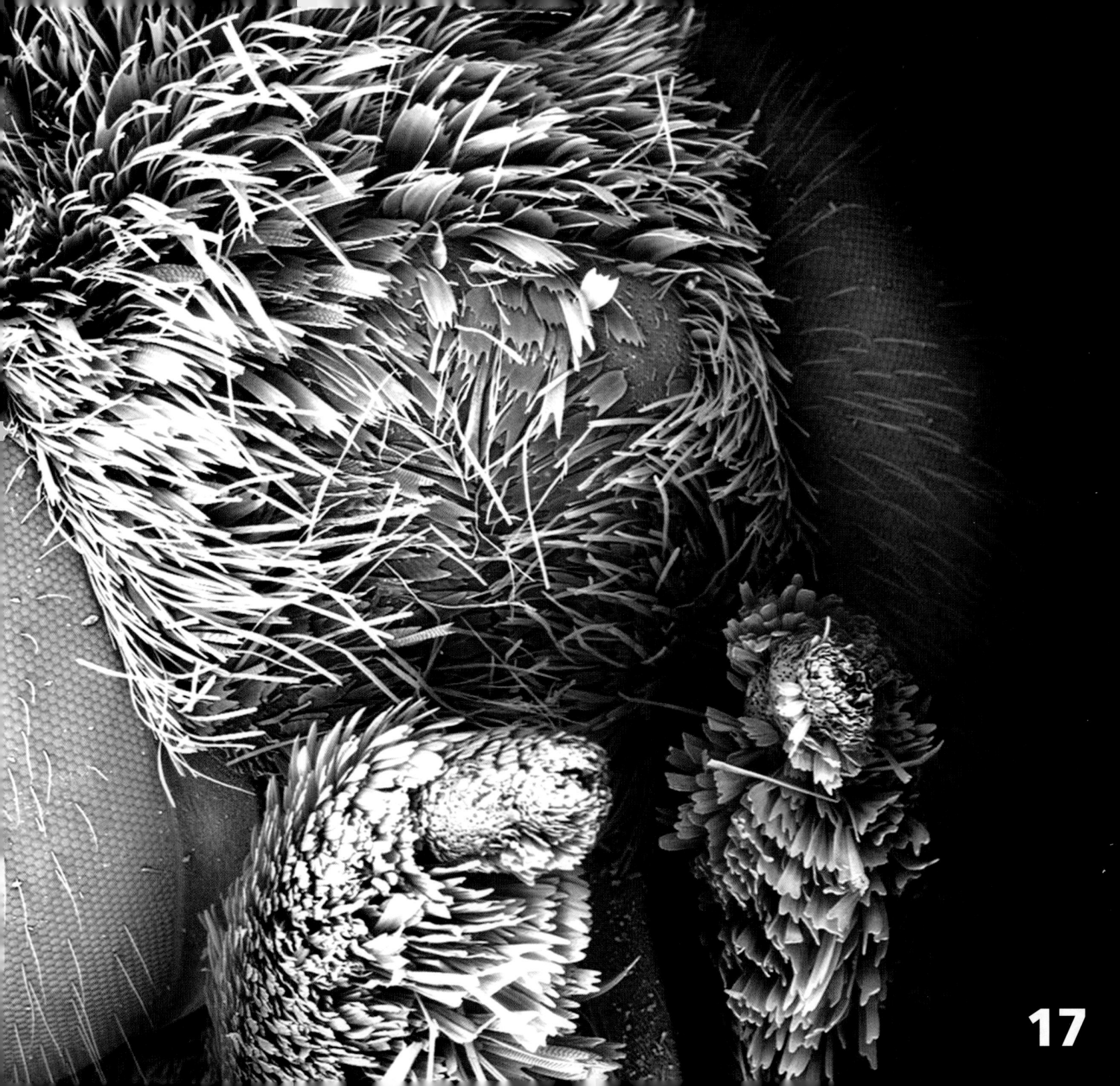

Moths have very long tongues.

They use their very long tongues to find food in flowers.

Moths are important in nature.

In nature, moths spread pollen between flowers.
This helps new flowers to grow.

21

MOTH FACTS

These pages provide more detail about the interesting facts found in the book. They are intended to be used by adults as a learning support to help young readers round out their knowledge of each insect or arachnid featured in the *Fascinating Insects* series.

Pages 4–5

Moths are flying insects that look like butterflies. Insects are small animals with six legs, segmented bodies, and hard outer shells called exoskeletons. Moths are part of the Lepidoptera order, which also includes butterflies. There are more than 150,000 species of moths. They can range in size from wingspans of 0.16 inches (4 millimeters) to about 1 foot (30 centimeters). Most moths are nocturnal, or active at night.

Pages 6–7

Moths live in most parts of the world. They live on every continent except Antarctica. Moths have adapted to life in a wide variety of environments, including forests, wetlands, scrub, chaparrals, mountains, deserts, and even tundra areas near the arctic. Some species are limited to small areas, while others spread out across entire continents. Most types of moths are found in tropic areas such as rainforests.

Pages 8–9

Moths are born when they hatch from eggs. Like butterflies, moths go through four stages of development as they grow: egg, larva, pupa, and adult. Shortly after mating, female moths begin laying eggs. Depending on the species, they may lay hundreds or even thousands of eggs at one time. Most moths lay their eggs on or near the kinds of plants the young hatchlings will need for food once they are born.

Pages 10–11

Moths are called caterpillars when they are young. In the larval, or caterpillar, stage, moths spend most of their time eating. This gives them the energy needed to grow and prepare to pupate. As they grow, caterpillars shed their skin four to five times. This is called molting. Most caterpillars do not leave the plants they were born on. Caterpillars do not have true eyes. They have small simple eyes that can only detect differences in light and dark.

Pages 12–13

Moth caterpillars wrap themselves in a bag of silk called a cocoon. When they are ready to enter the pupal stage, caterpillars spin a cocoon of silk around themselves. Inside the cocoon, the pupa goes through a process of change called metamorphosis. During this stage, the pupa changes into an adult moth, called an imago. Some types of moths bury themselves in the ground for this stage, while others hide under leaves or tree bark.

Pages 14–15

Moths have four wings when they are fully-grown. Adult moths have two large forewings and two smaller hind wings. For most moths, bristles on the bottom edge of the forewing connect to the hind wing, making the two wings work as one. The colors and patterns seen on the wings come from tiny scales and hairs that cover the wings. In addition to flying, the color patterns of the wings also help camouflage moths with plants in their environment.

Pages 16–17

Moths have two large eyes with many parts. They have two large compound eyes that can be made up of thousands of individual eye units, called ommatidia. These eyes give the moth great ability to detect motion, but they do not allow it to see distant objects clearly. Most moths have simple eyes, or ocelli. Instead of forming images, these eyes help moths detect differences in light and dark.

Pages 18–19

Moths have very long tongues. A moth's tongue is called a proboscis. It is coiled up close to its head when not in use. When in use, the proboscis straightens out to work like a straw. This allows moths to suck up liquids such as nectar from flowers. This is the only way adult moths can feed. Unlike caterpillars, most imago moths do not have mouths. Some moths do not even have a working proboscis. These moths only eat during the larval stage.

Pages 20–21

Moths are important in nature. When moths feed from the nectar of flowers, the short, bristly hairs that cover a moth's body, antennae, and wings pick up pollen from the flower. The moth then goes to another flower, where it deposits this pollen and picks up new pollen. This helps pollinate the flowers so they can reproduce. Since most moths are nocturnal, they are one of the most important pollinators for night-blossoming flowers. Moths also serve as food for larger animals, such as bats.

KEY WORDS

Research has shown that as much as 65 percent of all written material published in English is made up of 300 words. These 300 words cannot be taught using pictures or learned by sounding them out. They must be recognized by sight. This book contains 41 common sight words to help young readers improve their reading fluency and comprehension. This book also teaches young readers several important content words. These words are paired with pictures to aid in learning and improve understanding.

Page	Sight Words First Appearance
4	the
5	are, like, look, that
6	in, live, most, of, parts, to, world
8	from, they, when
9	long
10	young
11	their, time
12	a
13	grow, into
14	four, have
15	and, animals, other, use
16	eyes, help, large, many, see, two, with
18	very
19	find, food
20	between, important, new

Page	Content Words First Appearance
4	moth
5	butterflies, insects
6	areas
8	eggs
9	worms
10	caterpillars
12	bag, cocoon, silk
14	wings
16	dark
18	tongues
19	flowers
20	nature, pollen

Check out www.av2books.com for activities, videos, audio clips, and more!

1. Go to www.av2books.com.
2. Enter book code. Y376348
3. Fuel your imagination online!

www.av2books.com